CW01207198

The Rubáiyát of Dinky Dye of Vinegar Yard
Translated from the Cockney

Les Francis

Patchworks Publications

For Melanie and Emma

First published in this format 2024
All content copyright © 2024 Les Francis
Copyright © 1968 Les Francis

Les Francis asserts the moral right to be recognised as the author of this work

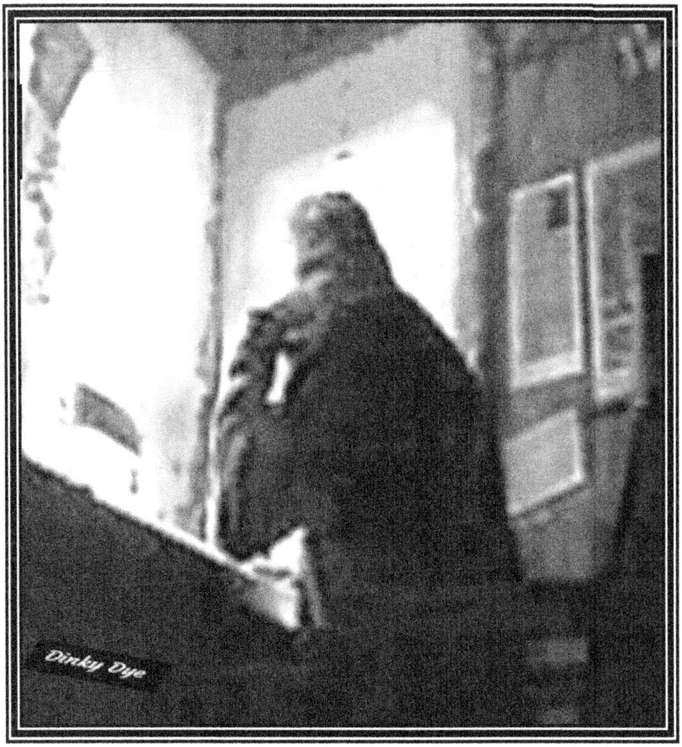
Dinky Dye

Vinegar Yard

Contents

Introduction and Background	7
THE RUBÁIYÁT OF DINKY DYE OF VINEGAR YARD	19
Afterword From Dinky Dye	57
A Brief Alphabet Of Cockney	59
Dinky Dye's Book Of 'Ditties'.	79
Index Of First Lines	81

The Rubáiyát of Dinky Dye of Vinegar Yard

INTRODUCTION AND BACKGROUND

The Borough was a lively, bustling throng; a busy and vibrant wholesale fruit and vegetable market by London Bridge, at the very heart of London town, just upstream of Tower Bridge and downstream of Blackfriars. The market was open for business from the early hours each weekday morn, right up through to the early afternoon. Then, the shutters would roll down. The earlier jostle and hustle and toing and froing of barrows piled so high with crates and boxes you would think they would surely fall off in a tumble or be just too much of a bulk to even move was gone; the streets were empty and the market abandoned, devoid of human interaction.

It would be left up to the salesmen: sometimes, they would close up early, sometimes later, all depending on the trade. They would all then trail off home while the clerks, who worked from nine to five, worked on – to take and bank the day's takings and, the stock taken and the books made up for the day, send off the reports to Covent Garden. Either way, when the day's work was done, they, too, would pack up and head off home. It was 'job and finish': plain and simple as that.

They were a grand sort who worked there, of blunt words, straight talking and rounded character. These were the very salt of the earth you could say and you would not be too far

The Rubáiyát of Dinky Dye of Vinegar Yard

wrong. All of that is now, alas, long gone and forgotten. A new culture has sprung up to replace the old. The market was just one of many, including meat and fish at Smithfield and Billingsgate, and there were other fruit and veg markets at Stratford, Spitalfields, and Covent Garden. This last, they moved eventually to Nine Elms.

The single most dominating feature at the Borough was the Cathedral and, coming out of London Bridge Station, its very grandeur struck you. There, at the very bottom of the concourse, yes, it actually struck you, not as a punch or a blow below the belt, but a resounding buck to uplift the heart by its very presence!

The imposing stone walls of Southwark Cathedral reached high, uplifting and proud. For nine long centuries or so it had stood there to provide solace and command reverence and respect, enduring the taxing depredation of time. It had survived the Blitz! Sad to say it, but this grandeur is now lost, its stature diminished and dwarfed by the Shard, a mile-high secular statement in glass, in whose shadow, now, it stands! Reduced to the apparent appearance of a child's doll's house toy, its previous impact on the eye is all gone forever.

Still, but enter within and its statement is yet uplifting to the soul, a memorial to what the exterior aspect once presented. From here, pilgrims once embarked upon their way to Canterbury, having already traipsed all the way from Winchester, the old capital of Wessex. Through the Itchen Valley and along the North Downs, they came, stopping off for lodging in towns and villages, from Farnham to Dorking and Reigate, perhaps, along their way.

The Rubáiyát of Dinky Dye of Vinegar Yard

Here, Becket set out. Here, also, did Shakespeare worship. Here, his younger brother, Edmund, was laid to rest. Here, a pilgrim through life, Dinky Dye once wended his way, down the steep stone steps, through the consecrated ground and on to find fresh market produce to retail on his stall amongst the local street markets.

He was a regular and familiar figure in the Borough. He knew the salesmen well and they him, holding him with a high regard and fond and mutually shared respect. He would make and have discreet arrangements of reciprocal commercial benefit with them, providing him with a goodly means to make a steady but honest living. At Dan Wuille's, most notably, and Samuel Bates and the Brothers Lee and others, Dinky Dye would trade and deal and shake hands on it.

At day's end, his produce sold, his transactions and dealings done and all accomplished to his general satisfaction, he dragged his weary feet straightway home for his tea or else, ofttimes seeking solace, found it in The Grapes with a fellow market crony he had fallen in with to talk and jest upon their day, of some happening or event that had caught their humour and their fancy.

A wholesale market still remains but a new culture has overtaken and taken over from the old. The down to earth, rough lot are all gone, sent packing, a relic of past times to mull upon and ponder. A retail market for fine cuisine has been established and traders trade as trade must to find and fill their own special niche of opportunity. Fine, new upmarket restaurants for the genteel and other specialist

The Rubáiyát of Dinky Dye of Vinegar Yard

food shops for the discerning, everywhere, sprawl now, inside and alongside, next to the old market, to cater to the new clientele it has become a venue and attraction for. It is more now a meeting place and public attraction for the hospitality trade.

London itself, it appears, has a new culture and a population with new passions to satisfy. Newcomers have come, from far afield and far and wide, and made here a new home for themselves, bringing new customs, new demands, and new wares to trade and share and acquaint and familiarise others with.

Here, locally produced and organic food with a weekend gourmet market is now available, while a committee of stallholders and trustees, so it appears, now manages responsibility for upkeep, ensuring that standards are kept and maintained. Wine and cocktail bars abound. It is all such a contrast to how things once were – a common place for common folk to trade and do business.

Dinky Dye would not recognise it at all for sure. These London streets have ever been a cultural soup, its flavours acquired from centuries of global trade and commerce and those also seeking sanctuary and protection against some new foreign tyranny on the continent. The exotic produce now available on sale would also be an oddity, but an economic opportunity he would quickly recognise and seize!

Would he approve? Would he disapprove? He would pass no comment, perhaps, but accept his humble place before the immutable march of time. One of that rough lot but a sparkling diamond inside, he would acknowledge that our time and our brief presence felt upon these London thoroughfares is as fleeting as the waters' lap upon the muddy banks that confine Old Father Thames.

Both sage and raconteur, his earthy insights were renown amongst the company of all sorts that were his acquaintance. A pint of ale was quite enough and would let loose and unrein his quicksilver tongue with a flood of banter. Veins of cinnabar ran through Dinky Dye's mortal frame, so quick was his wit and with a humour to match besides! The Grapes would shake its very boards with hearty laughter, encouraging a response to almost equal his droll observations on their life and times. Ears would prick and those other patrons present, quite enjoying their own good company, not one amongst the merry band of his consort, would harken to the calling of their interest to join in or listen.

This was Dinky Dye. His day complete, he would make himself the heart and soul of those assembled he made his congregation! To any and all the fine fellow-me-lads who may have been there present, he was a shining star in their midst, orbiting their very heaven for them to look up to and aspire to, some day, be his very equal.

Traipsing back home after, with a song on his lips and a hymn in his heart, he would ponder upon the travails and mysteries of the life that beset his every day, celebrating his good fortune to earn a living sufficient to sustain himself and his loved ones. He expected nothing, demanded not anything, asked only the good Lord may provide for him enough to sustain him another day and provide for his beloved family.

His good lady wife his sweetheart had been and had made a go of it with him for all those past twenty and seven years, bearing him the three children he loved dearly. They were used to his habit of cavorting with his cronies, accepting his wont willingly. Coming through the door with a cheerful whistle to greet them, he would leave the day's takings on the table for her to deal with. She, likewise, would have all prepared for him. He loved his sprats fried in a batter served up for tea and she would have them waiting ready for him on the hot plate. The table would be laid and she would join him with a pot of tea to discuss their day.

Dinky Dye was a man of most particular culinary taste and would travel all the way down to Brixton town just for a meal in the pie and mash shop there. He would take an upstairs table by favour every time. It would be a special treat for them all – his family, too – served up as he liked it, with a rich, brown gravy, a generous helping of 'parsley' (a common white sauce laced well with chopped fresh parsley) and a good splash of 'non-brewed' (vinegar) to top it off for flavour. He would place his order and patiently await the dumb waiter to bring it up, served up by the attendant waitress. There'd be smiles all round for sure at the hearty meal and everyone would tuck in with a zeal!

His thoughts had always been a-buzz thinking up his 'ditties' as he liked to call them. Everything rhymed for Dinky Dye. He loved playing with words and playing cards and loved his

The Rubáiyát of Dinky Dye of Vinegar Yard

Cribbage. He would even have to make a rhyme or two of the scoring! "Fifteen-two and that'll do!" or, "One for his nob'll do the job!" he would chirrup with a hearty smile that stretched clean across from cheek to shining cheek! If he cut a Jack, it would ever extract from those quick lips a cry of, "Two for his heels, I'll have jellied eels!" and that would, without fail, plant a grin on all who shared the table!

Only in later years did he take to writing his 'ditties' down and make a record of them in orderly fashion. He kept a desk by the window in the small boxroom. His 'business desk' he called it, where he did his accounts for the taxman. Here, he would sit and ponder his day at the end of the day and took to writing them all down, just for his own personal amusement and pleasure.

At the very first, it was just on scraps of paper he recorded them. These he kept safe in his desk drawer. This was not a tidy state of affairs and, later, Dinky Dye collected them all together in a little black notebook purchased especially for that very purpose from the W. H. Smiths stationer's shop in the Elephant and Castle. As the inclination so took him, he would jot them down and add to them and so the collection grew.

His eldest son, George, out of affectionate praise, took to calling him the 'Borough Bard'! "Well," he would chortle with a hearty laugh, "Wasn't Shakespeare himself once a parishioner at the cathedral?" This seemed to please Dinky Dye readily and he began to think better of his humble efforts than he had done so previously and actually thought in terms of their publication. It was just a thought, no more,

The Rubáiyát of Dinky Dye of Vinegar Yard

but there was another who took the thought more seriously and gave it sincere attention.

George had lots of contacts. 'Networking', I believe, is what they would call it today. Ever diplomatic and tactful, subtlety was George's middle name. Having given the matter most particular thought and careful consideration of how best to proceed without arousing the Old Man's curiosity as to his intentions, he actually proceeded with his plan.

George had settled on the straightforward approach of simply asking the Old Man if he could have a read of his 'ditties' and the Old Man happily obliged. George took them off instead to a printer he knew down Whitechapel High Street and had several small booklets printed off and bound for the family. When presented with his copy, Dinky Dye was quite taken aback and, well, quite over the moon!

Dinky Dye's days at the Borough – like everyone else's – were, already, numbered. The beginning of the end of what was there and finally saw off the old Borough Market was the appearance of the supermarket on the High Street. Dinky Dye saw this for himself when the Pricerite Buyers began to put in their appearance in the Borough, buying in huge quantities of produce in bulk.

Traders, traditionally, had been small businesses such as the small shops and restaurants of the immediate and wider area. A typical High Street would see dozens of small shops offering every range of wares, from the fishmongers to the grocers and greengrocers, all of which were swallowed up by what is now on offer in the supermarkets. Morrison's

The Rubáiyát of Dinky Dye of Vinegar Yard

'Market Street' attempts to replicate this in-store but cannot replace it.

How did they start? Where did they begin? At Grove Park, in South London, a supermarket was literally constructed across the very railway line, next to the station. These supermarkets are become superstores and now have their own arrangements, actually purchasing direct from the growers, bypassing, sidestepping the markets altogether. If that is a good thing or no for fair competition is a matter for debate – or, perhaps, it isn't! All manner of factors affect the price of bread but I well remember the price of a large Bloomer going up from eleven pence ha'penny to one and a ha'penny and my Old Lady went through the roof: "What, more than a shilling for a loaf of bread!" Still, the old state of affairs went and, over a period, the new has taken over and it hasn't saved us a single penny.

Is the new better than the old; was the old worse than what has replaced it? Dinky Dye, in his heart of hearts, would say a definitive and hearty 'No' to that! What, greens and spuds wrapped up in plastic? No! Spuds were sold loose, washed or unwashed; the unwashed, with earth still clinging to them, were sold the cheaper for it! Now, they tell us the world's drowning in plastic. 'Small wonder,' Dinky Dye would have said. As for plastic bin bags for rubbish, he would have said, 'Rubbish!' to that, too. Your rubbish goes straight in the bin and it's carted off and that's that!

One of his uncles had been a rag and bone man in his time, doing his rounds with his horse and cart around Brixton. Where're there's muck there's money, so they do say, and

The Rubáiyát of Dinky Dye of Vinegar Yard

this was free enterprise at its most enterprising. He would ring his hand bell, calling out: "Rag, bone!" and housewives would answer the call to their doors with their offerings. For the better items, he'd reward them with a goldfish out the tank he carried on board with him. They would be worth a bob or two! The kids would plead with their mums to throw out the old clothes for that!

This was 'recycling' in a world that had never heard of recycling and 'Green' politics! Old rags were used to make paper. Even old rope could be used to make a coarse paper. It was all money for old rope, you might say. Bones were used to make glue and a pigment called ivory-black. Cinders, too, could be used for making bricks and the residue for mending the roads. Any old iron would also be a premium! Times change and life moves on. The rag and bone men had had their day.

They were replaced by the dustmen and their totting carts! That's what became the real issue and was at the heart of the great dustbin strike. It was at the close of that decade – when England swung like a pendulum do, as Roger Miller had lyrically put it – that the London Councils stepped in to end this little 'free enterprise' enterprise. The dustmen walked out!

Dinky Dye's brother-in-law, Ron, walked out with the rest of them when they went on strike in Hackney. They were all going to lose the free cash they'd earnt, all 'totted up' between them at the end of every week. The crews were going to have none of that, of course. They were going to put in for a substantial pay rise to compensate. Labour and

The Rubáiyát of Dinky Dye of Vinegar Yard

Tory: they were all the same, just wanting control. The householder would pass them some 'beer money' and that old bedstead would be carted away in a trice! Now, the councils charge the householder goodness knows what, it's no wonder there's fly-tipping!

Dinky Dye put together some lines and his son, George, had them printed off for him. Together, he and Ron handed them out to explain the issues of what it was all about. It all dragged on and it didn't all end entirely well, but that seems to be in the way of the world. Time moves on and, unless you move on with it, you get left behind. But, at least, Dinky Dye has left behind his 'Ditties'!

The Rubáiyát of Dinky Dye of Vinegar Yard

THE RUBÁIYÁT OF DINKY DYE OF VINEGAR YARD

1.

First light of morn slinks through the tattered blind –
The light, insistent, filters in – ne'er mind!
   She stirs from slumber – dally? – Nay, be gone!
Leave thought of such indulgencies behind!

2

Day breaks, the market calls and I depart –
The traders muster, haggle, bargain, bart
   For sale or purchase – contracts, matters far
More pressing than transactions of the heart!

3

As morn's chance slingshot glances off St. Paul's,
The dome of night is rent with greeting calls –
   The cash-till rattle of the shutters thrills!
And salesmen stand attentive at their stalls!

4

Their market wares all set out on display,
The market traders start another day;
   The porters stand, alert, in readiness
To cart the purchase off to load the dray.

5

The Borough comes alive with commerce and
With traffic thronged; and we – this happy band! –
   Begin another week, another day,
As happy as the sandboys in the sand!

6

How happy I, my produce sold, return
To profit from the profit that I earn
   And spend an hour in pleasant company
The Grapes provides – or do I money burn!

7

Nay, 'tis not so – good company I share
With fellows of like trade and like affair!
   Such bonhomie and hospitality –
An hour may easy pass to two, I swear!

8

When small ado is much a-being done
And, without consequence, we bond as one
   In merriment – spill out our very souls
Carousing! – then, as one we are – or none!

9

When life is but a bitter Chalice, then
Take for yourself a tankard – two – or ten!
  Each must seek out his consolation, we
Who are but flotsam and but mortal men!

10

Ought is there that may last? Nay, there is nought –
Time is the net ensnares us – we are caught!
  That fisher man of men laughs at us – all!
And, "Time!" the Landlord calls, as he is ought!

11

Deserted is the market, shuttered up,
And we are all turned out – we had our sup
  And now, all merry but the worse for wear –
Our very souls spilt out – we are an empty cup!

12

Across in yon Cathedral grounds, I vouch
The vagrants huddle there – yes, there they crouch –
   Upon the benches that serve as their beds!
A boon, I toss them: Rizlas from my pouch.

13

"God bless you, Guv'nor," is their stock response.
Oft times have I affected nonchalance,
   Yet taken them aloft to purchase some
Tobacco – as a comfort to ensconce!

14

By choice as much by circumstance they live;
By choice as much by circumstance I give!
   It is a pleasure for them who have none –
And, out of every dram, the dregs must sieve!

The Rubáiyát of Dinky Dye of Vinegar Yard

15

Abroad the Borough High Street, there, I stroll
And think on things – significant, not droll –
   A Christian act it is, not politic,
To gladly give of what I have as dole!

16

Of all the virtues, acts of charity –
To share and share alike twixt you and me,
   To give and to receive – it is not strained
But falls like rain from heav'n, not forced, but free!

17

A blessing, then, upon us both it is –
The Christian to extol his virtue 'tis
   And for the supplicant so to receive
The benefaction granted that is his!

18

Give out of generosity than take
Out of resentment – nobler does it make
   Us! – Take from others so to give what's theirs?
Nay, Christian, giving's for the giving's sake!

19

The day's been long and taken of its toll
But solitude's oft solace for the soul –
   Observer, not participant, I watch
The world rush by – a fish amongst the shoal!

20

Small steps lead ever on to greater strides!
Proud moments lead to great achievements – pride's
   Not vanity nor fall that's tempered so –
Mulled by humility and recognised!

21

The music of the Market's fresh still in my ear –
The clicks and rattles of the hoist – such cheer
   As friendly banter's shared and, then, the crash
Of cases – Pearmains stacked up in a tier!

22

Good days, good times, times past and times of ole
I dwell upon and take my homeward stroll –
   Regrets? I have a few but they are nought
Compared my ought endeavours as a whole!

23

Yet, closer do I look, less do I see
And less substantial all appears to be –
   Was all a dream within a dream and I
The dreamer? Was it? – So, it seems to me!

24

Some say it's so – life is a simple game!
Then, bear not grudge that others might bear blame
   But grant your father's name some good repute –
That others may not sully or defame.

25

And let us leave it better than we find,
A proud remembrance that we leave behind,
   And know we were a beacon light to guide –
A paradigm for others to remind.

26

Time's not misspent – nay, say it isn't so –
That's passed in tryst, a lover with her beau!
   Time's fleeting, here and gone – Take heart
For, soon enough, it's gone before you know.

27

Ah, youth is sweet – no more these foul laments –
'Tis time for love's, sweet love's entanglements!
  Time then to learn the wisdom of the wise
There is – or learn it by experience!

28

Heed well and take the path that Wisdom takes,
And make not those mistakes that Folly makes.
  Learn well the lessons Wisdom has to teach,
Or learn them as he learned them – from mistakes!

29

But them that claim to be infallible –
Believe them not; else suffer them, a fool,
  In thinking that infallibility
Would be conferred on mortal man at all!

30

If I mistaken am by this or not,
We must be part of some mistaken plot,
   I think, that error ever plagues us so.
Ah, then – by what mistake were we begot!

31

Not mere experience, but wisdom that
Has been learned by experience and what
   Life is makes perfect. Pray bear this in mind
As you read this poor verse of Rubáiyát!

32

Experience imperfect wisdom brings
For, in His wisdom, He made human things
   Imperfect – that we would on Him depend?
Nay, learn – that life, a bed of nettles, stings!

The Rubáiyát of Dinky Dye of Vinegar Yard

33

Leave not the fancies of the heart to fly
For, like a butterfly, they flutter by
   To sojourn for a little while – then pass
Like dreams lost in the very night – and die.

34

Now is the time, now is the time to live,
Now, to enjoy life – and how else but with
   Some pleasant female company – that, chance,
Will promise not to be too talkative!

35

Ah, not for nothing do you give your love
To her – and the anticipation of
   Her love, that is not all you love her for –
Nor is it for the cooing coos the dove!

36

Some say – "It is not loving that destroys
The soul – a love that but with loving toys
　It is will cause more hurt and heartache." Pray
Deliver my poor heart from maudlin Troys!

37

I drew my heavy heart from out my breast
And laid him down beside the flowers to rest
　That, chance, he may become alike the flowers –
And he might flower like them like him close-pressed.

38

Ah, foolishness! A heart is not a flower,
Though governed by the selfsame Godly power
　It is and, like the flowers, my heart was plucked,
A trophy to adorn my lady's bower!

39

Yes, this one toyed with love and left forlorn
The heart to which his heart his love had sworn
   That when he gave his heart in love again,
Ah, this was how love treated him – with scorn!

40

But love intoxicates as does the vine –
As to the grape you shall yourself resign
   To her! She flatters you that she is yours
But you are hers –and that is her design.

41

As does the vine cleave to the pole, you cleave
To her and swear your all you'll never leave!
   Love leaves you witless – fool! – entangled! 'Tis
A web of self-deception do you weave.

42

A stolen kiss – how like a dream dreamt 'tis –
How like a dream his love he thought was his
   But, once that she has won him for her own,
How then she takes for granted sympathies.

43

First love, first kiss – a dream, a prize to seize –
'Twill surely bring him to his very knees!
   So does he yearn to win his lady's hand,
A merry dance she leads him if you please!

44

Beware! Else shall you certain come to grief –
For love shall tug your foolish heart, frail leaf,
   And tear it free – and, buffeted just so,
Shall steal away your heart, that surly thief!

45

Once to the wind of love your heart is thrown
Then, never more, your thoughts will be your own.
   Your head will call you this way and your heart –
Well, he will call you that though you bemoan.

46

Life's story can be written on a page –
Alas, too soon, sweet youth is soured by age
   And beauty's fascination passes soon –
Too soon as, actors, we depart the stage!

47

Frail human flesh we are: we come and go!
Is love eternal? Say that it is so –
That, though we exit, our performance done,
Some ought of us lives on as, leaves, we blow!

48

So poorly our performance is received
By that Eternal Audience that heaved
   Us from the womb to do as we might do?
Nay, make not such complaint; be not sore-grieved!

49

For Him who judges us, He says we could
To His design have fashioned of the wood;
   Instead, we whittle down our lives to nought,
For ought and everything but that we should!

50

Old Death creeps up on us and, ere our time
Is up, he grabs us – just as we are prime
   For plucking! And he plucks us – loved ones, all,
And all of us fall victim to his crime.

51

When that one sends his frenzied pack, his horde
Of Fates, to hunt us down, with bloodied sword
　To run us through, that no-one may escape –
He cuts down both the servant and the lord.

52

Death, that usurper of Life's throne, is chased
Throughout our lives we live in wanton haste;
　And all we say is, "All we need is time!"
But that one spares no time for us to waste.

53

Death does not leave the last bloom on the stem –
The very first nor very last of them!
　He leaves us lonely, desolate, alone,
Then takes us, also, without an – 'Ahem'!

54

A bitter wine it is to taste of – life! –
But life is precious, though it brings us strife;
   Scent not too deeply of the flowers, then – love's
A drug – and you may end up with a wife!

55

How sweet is that first kiss – so does it seem
And love the long fulfilment of a dream!
   Why, if you don't about you keep your wits,
A fool she'll make you, wrapped up by her scheme!

56

But fools believe in love – they will not learn!
Still, we who have our wits about us yearn
   To fall in love like that, love and be loved,
To give and want back nothing in return!

57

Is love, then, for the simple and naïve?
Is it conceit persuades us to believe
   That someone could love us? – How willingly,
False heart, deceived, you would yourself deceive!

58

Love, that blind reason of our hearts, invents
Such hopes, such dreams, small wonder that our sense
   Of judgement is unbalanced and, between
This and true reason, knows no difference!

59

Sleep on young lovers in your dream of bliss,
Dream on those dreams of your first and last kiss –
   Wake not for, if your first kiss be your last,
Your hearts will break and surely come amiss!

60

Of loves sweet memories so few remain –
Love, like the lady moon, must wax – and wane!
   Perhaps love will allow but time will not
That, once love is lost, we shall love again!

61

But let the heart be summoned by desire
And we may to loves promise yet aspire –
   But only let loves sweet encounters fan
The flame of love to set the heart afire!

62

Whose lips have once desired his truelove's lips;
Who yearns to taste the wine of love – and sips:
   The centre-light of reason in his mind,
In loves intoxication, will eclipse!

63

Ah, why must reason from good sense depart
And from our minds that we, who know no art,
  No guile to counter that of love, are left
Dependent on the judgement of – the heart?

64

Fool, still does he believe although she lies
And, though that light of judgement, Reason, tries
  To guide him yet aright, he heeds not – though
Experience has taught him otherwise!

65

What hope is there for us then when a smile
May win away our reason, so beguile
  Us that it seems we want to be beguiled
And readily fall for a woman's wile?

66

Fools we must be, then, else we must be mad
To throw away what peace of mind we had
   For love – but, without love, there is no sense
No purpose and no meaning life may add.

67

Can it be that experience has lied –
Or that we are deceived by some false pride,
   Embittered by the way love treated us?
Experience cannot be typified!

68

So, too, can it be said for life, that we
Are swayed more by how things appear to be
   Than rather how they really are and, then,
But seeing only that we want to see.

69

Ah, life is not so easily defined –
And never so we mortal creatures find
   True understanding of it, but the wise –
Them that just think they know or them well-wined!

70

Leave them to argue out amongst themselves
For each into the depths of wisdom delves,
   Each as a child into this riddle – life,
As we into the riddle of ourselves.

71

What merit then is there in wisdom or
That little which they own to have? Ignore
   Them! – We might just as well judge for ourselves:
They are as wise as we are on this score!

72

When we were young we yearned to be as wise
As were our elders: that we could surprise
   Them wisdom such as that they had was ours –
Ah, youth we had, by far the greater prize!

73

While you are young, then, live, enjoy your youth:
Them that need proof of things and seek some truth
   Or measure of it overlook the one
Truth – love! Live, ere you're grown old in the tooth!

74

Ah, leave them with their futile search and come
With Dinky Dye whose heart beats like a drum
   The two strong beats of truth and love, ere of
The bread of life there is not left a crumb!

75

Why this concern with death and human fate
When down each unknown passageway they wait
   Within the shadow of misfortune? Make
The most of life before it is too late!

76

Love and give all the love you have to give;
Engage not in such discourse, combative:
   Waste not your life away on matters such,
Exploring puzzles so complex – just live!

77

Live life for living's sake and fear not Death,
That He will overtake your every breath –
   Live now! The flower of youth life weaves to make
Her garland fair Death takes to make a wreath!

78

Leave it not so late as this fool has done,
Who wished for sunshine when he had the sun,
   Who truth sought, love and wished that they were his
To win a heart for him when it was won!

79

In life, do we seek meaning and embark
Upon life's journey, ignorant and – hark!
   Death summons us before we know and then,
Ah, then the truth is all too plain and stark!

80

Wherever life leads, there must we be led!
Ah mourn not for this one when he is dead:
   He wished away his time and now he has
None left he wishes it all back instead!

81

Times come, times pass, ere done, leave us behind!
What mark we make, if brought we are to mind,
   Then, let it be through favour than fraught blot
On copybook, and nothing underlined!

82

Old Father Thames, they say, keeps rolling on;
From on his many bridges – there upon,
   Our lots we cast onto his murky drink
And watched them swim away until they'd gone!

83

Old Father Time, too, marches he along –
And kingdoms come, according to the song,
   And kingdoms go; whate'er the end may be,
He's deaf to all the clamour of the throng!

84

Despite entreaties to him with us while,
Our protestations just add to the pile –
  He waits for none: he's here and on his way –
What's ours of his leaks out through tap and spile!

85

Aye, tap and spile! Small wonder, then, if we
Indulge in dalliance! Come you, then, with me
  And we shall, "Landlord!" call for one last round
And happy for a little more shall be!

86

The more I take this maze of life apart,
The more illusion does appear each part –
  The closer look, look I, less do I see;
The harder is the stock of it to chart!

87

Then, what is life: is all for all or nought?
The whither of it, erstwhile, sages sought!
   Is then, as sages say, life but a dream,
A nurse's rhymes as little babes are taught?

88

Am I a stranger in a stranger's land?
My father's and my father's father's hand
   Before bore me my birthright coster's trade –
Here, I belong, still, maudlin stamps its brand.

89

May it be so, a dream, as does it seem?
Ah, me, then seems, within a dream I dream
   And ply my trade, a Costermonger's life,
A simple man of simple self-esteem!

90

There, what know I of this or ought about,
 A man of simple deed and little clout?
  Of little note am I but this I note –
That what's not found within you go without!

91

Time waits not, cares not, neither deaf nor blind,
But summons us, so mark what's left behind
  Stands as a monument proud to preserve
A stature of repute to all remind.

92

In truth they say, in truth, so it is said:
Do much, do well – you are a long time dead!
  Love, laugh, make hay and shine – yes, surely shine
Ere has the sun the vault of heaven fled!

93

If all be well, of good repute our name,
And all is to our credit, not our shame,
   With not a blot upon our copybook
And nothing underlined that might defame,

94

Then, we may know we did our level best
And we have pulled our weight like all the rest
   And played our part, yes, to the very full –
Whate'er the outcome, we have stood the test!

95

What may be so and, to our knowledge, know
To be so may not be undone – 'tis so!
   Move on, accept what is: 'tis surely done
What is – acceptance is the salve of woe!

96

All's but a construct of the mind – just that!
There, all's begun; all's but a thought begat!
   Was not creation, so it's said, begun
So, with a Word? There, then, so 'tis thereat!

97

Hard times some may encounter, some may not:
Our character is tested – 'tis our lot!
   Whatever is our circumstance or state,
If not ourselves, then we have nothing got!

98

Sun, rise; Moon, set: another day begins –
The world, a-rush, upon its axis spins!
   Days come, days go and Time waits not – nor we!
Somewhere, I heard it said that, "Who dares wins!"

The Rubáiyát of Dinky Dye of Vinegar Yard

99

Another day to do with what we can –
The new morn greets us with no gainsay than
   We do our most and do the best we may
And make more with the day than it began.

100

You see the road before you: then, keep on,
Along the road that you've set out upon –
   Who wins, who loses? Nay, it matters not,
For nought defeats us save our faith is gone.

101

Until the very end, without regard,
Work long and, ever with a will, work hard
   And waver not from your intended course –
Stout heart! Be true! For what is starred is starred.

102

Begin each day with kindly thought anew;
Act righteously, act honestly and true!
  Did not the Dock Green Bobby always say
That honesty's best policy to do?

103

The day's begun cloaked in a shroud of haze –
Across the Thames, it lingers long and stays!
  Believe! The portent's good; the mantle lifts –
Here, look you, shining through: the sun's ablaze!

104

The morn we have been walking has been long;
Too long, the overcast persisted, strong
  And lurked without relent! Our new day will
Soon come! Bear up; bear with it with a song!

105

Do they not say to whistle while you work?
Charged for a wasty price, I pay the clerk!
   Work with a will I shall and sell my wares:
"Here, Navels, Pearmains, all but for a perk!"

106

With hearty spirit and light-hearted trill,
The Costermongers cries yell loud and shrill!
   The ten bob notes soon change up for the pounds
And pennies pay the punters for the bill!

107

There, was it not all worth it? Play your part!
Just make yourself a living: play it smart
   And don't expect the world to owe you one
And don't upset the golden apple cart!

108

I've said my bit; I've said it all and more!
Here, Landlord, lock and bar the tavern door
   And long into the night we shall debate
Whatever's said – it's all been said before!

109

Then, fill my glass again and, one more time,
Define whence reason comes from, whence comes
      Rhyme,
   For, in defiance of all rationale,
My whispered words caressed those lips sublime!

110

Mark, when morn comes oft shrouded in a mist,
Walk garbed in Hope's apparel – don't desist!
   Our new day will soon come – have faith, believe!
And we'll carouse The Grapes, yet, Brahms and Liszt!

The Rubáiyát of Dinky Dye of Vinegar Yard

AFTERWORD FROM DINKY DYE

Sometimes, you may wonder how you have arrived at the person you have become. Then, perhaps, you begin to understand that the trauma and suffering you have endured contributed to the person you have become. Then, the jigsaw of life begins to piece together.

It is all a life's work. May it yet gain us wisdom.

The Rubáiyát of Dinky Dye of Vinegar Yard

The Rubáiyát of Dinky Dye of Vinegar Yard

A BRIEF ALPHABET OF COCKNEY

This isn't wholly about rhyming slang but the South London slang I grew up with and words and phrases that creep and sneak into colloquial language. It isn't even about the back slang adopted by street gangs and traders to speak amongst themselves privately by removing the initial letter, reversing the syllable and adding a conjunctive syllable to the end! A surviving word in popular use is 'Yob' or 'Yobbo' for a disruptive and unruly youngster. There was an enterprising grocer who used to ply our local streets with his brothers selling his wares off the back of his lorry. He would walk in front announcing his approach with what sounded like "Yahob, Orha Yahob!" which I imagined was back slang but could never decipher it!

The modern influence is more through US film, video and television and, lately, that used online. The way language is now more cadenced and nuanced is most noticeable I find. Amongst the young, the use of expressions such as - "I'm like...", "And I'm like...", "So I was like..." as a connective to bring a conversation to its leading point are all acquired from exposure to these sources.

Historically, this has always been the case, with the Norman French source, 'assault' and the identical English source, 'battery', both becoming conjoined to form the offence of

The Rubáiyát of Dinky Dye of Vinegar Yard

'assault and battery' for instance. While there are legal distinctions between the two words, they essentially mean the same thing but stem from dual usage through the period of transition back to English under Henry IV, the first English speaking monarch after William I (the Conqueror).

With the regular influx of newcomers seeking betterment or sanctuary, spoken English, most readily and enthusiastically, adopted new words. Words like kosher from the Yiddish have been adopted, to mean okay, above board or the real thing. The Empire brought home words like juggernaut, from the huge vehicle which was hauled through the streets during religious festivals bearing an image of Krishna; pukka meaning genuine or authentic; and expressions like a 'cup of char' for a cup of tea, all derived from the Hindi. 'Blighty' comes from the Hindi billayati, meaning a foreign land. British soldiers, sailors, airmen would wishfully and wistfully speak of getting back home to 'Good Old Blighty' (Great Britain), that far-off, foreign land.

To 'Take a Decko' or 'Have a Decko' is a slang expression that means to take a look at something. This phrase, too, originates from a Hindi word – dekho, which means look. The phrase 'Have a Shufty' comes from the Arabic word 'shufti' which means 'have you seen?' This word was brought into the English language by British soldiers serving in the Middle East and is used as a slang expression for 'take a look'.

English eagerly and readily adopts and adapts. Thus, 'How far!' – a familiar Nigerian greeting accompanied by a raised slap of the palm of the hands – became, 'High five!'

The Rubáiyát of Dinky Dye of Vinegar Yard

Likewise, in the same manner that English adopts a foreign tongue, the tongue has been readily adapted by the foreign user in Pidgin. Thus, 'Kumbaya': 'Come by here'. In the Book of Amos, the Lord repeats twice: "I will not again pass by them anymore."

Word association provided descriptive names for trades such as 'spark' for an electrician and 'chippy' for a carpenter or joiner. Shortening, also, provided descriptive names, like 'chippy' for a fish and chip shop and 'artic' for an articulated vehicle. The contraction of the greeting, 'What cheer!' became 'Wotcher!' and, of course, 'Well Come' became 'Welcome!'

Navvy became a general term for a labourer, from the navigators who built the canals, roads and railways. Many of these, although by no means all, would be recruited from Irish migrants speaking their own tongue. Other newcomer migrants, too, would talk amongst themselves in their own language or dialect and it was this, supposedly, which prompted such a response amongst the indigenous London locals as the construction of a 'counter tongue', or 'code' if you wish, in order that they, too, might enter into conversations amongst themselves, likewise, private and personal.

A greeting such as 'Me Old Cock Sparrer' (or sparrow) would serve as a salutation for a chirpy young chap or acquaintance. Hence: 'Wotcher Cock!' would be a derivative of this - from 'Cock Sparrow' - as a greeting or salutation of endearment. This would oft invite a rejoinder of 'Wotcher Mate!' - A mate, being a friend of fond

The Rubáiyát of Dinky Dye of Vinegar Yard

acquaintance, deriving, by association, from the expressive 'straight and narrow' and 'straight as an arrow' for a good and honest associate to rely upon.

'Titfer' is the slang for hat and derives from 'Tit for Tat' - hat - which, likewise, derives from 'This for That' - meaning a most just and righteous negative exchange! Although, some do suggest another connotation with fencing or duelling parlance and the expression, 'Tip for Tap' for its origins.

This, of course, leads in to the expression, 'Going Tats'. This is a contraction of 'Going Tat-tas' - as in: "Are we going out for a walk?" 'Tat-tas' comes from the fact that, when you were going out, you would say "Tat-ta" as in "Goodbye" which eventually evolved into the expression used for the action of going out. When you went out, it would be a habit or custom to don a hat and so we come full circle from 'Tit for Tat' (hat) to 'Tatty-bye' to say, "Goodbye"!

'Ta' is informal parlance for 'Thanks' or 'Thankyou' which some suggest stems from the Old Norse. You might say, 'Thanks' to your host when you depart their company. A single 'Ta' or 'Ta-a' is sometimes used as a shortened version of 'Tat-ta,' in the same way that "goodbye" might be shortened to "bye" which is also articulated as, "bye-bye!" This also translates as something quite different when said to a young child and expressed in the context of "going bye-byes!" Then, it takes on the meaning of going to sleep. This sense is not entirely separate or disparate in that there is a congruence or equivalence in 'parting company'.

The Rubáiyát of Dinky Dye of Vinegar Yard

During the Second Great War, 'Tat-ta for now' was adopted as the very famous catch-phrase used in the widely popular ITMA (It's That Man Again) programme on the BBC - recited by the cleaning lady, who was appropriately named Mrs Mopp, as she departed the company of Tommy Handly, the programme's host. This, also, is closely related by suggestion to 'Going Tats' - implying taking your leave, departing or going out. That leads back, full circle, once more, to where we were.

The now renowned saying of the Cockney Charlady, Mrs. Mopp (played by Dorothy Summers), was adapted into the initial letters, 'T.T.F.N.' - a contraction and acronym of 'Tat-ta for now' with which she bade her departure. 'TTFN' became widely used, migrating out of English English into American English, and being adopted by Endora, the witch, played by Agnes Moorehead in the ABC TV series, 'Bewitched', for instance, and used even in the Disney adaptation of Winnie the Pooh!

'Titfer' (slang for hat) deriving from 'Tit for Tat' - and 'tit' being slang for 'breast' - may explain the more recent use of 'Ta-tas' or 'Tatas' to mean breasts. Following a much publicised breast-cancer campaign in 2004, a foundation was established in the US with the name 'Save the Ta-tas' which sold promotional t-shirts with the slogan printed across the front. So does one expression, by association, derive from another; is shortened by derivative contraction - and may, eventually, be applied to something else, quite different and disparate from the original definition.

Terms of endearment become clipped, also, and shortened.

The Rubáiyát of Dinky Dye of Vinegar Yard

So, 'Duchess' which was an affectionate salutation for wife, especially in a relationship of long standing, was contracted to 'Dutch'. This, of course, is immortalised in that well-known song composed by the Music Hall performer, Albert Chevalier –

> "We've been together now for forty years,
> An' it don't seem a day too much,
> There ain't a lady livin' in the land
> As I'd swop for my dear Old Dutch."

Apart from the aforementioned, 'Wotcher Cock!' and the familiar rejoinder of, 'Wotcher Mate!' there are further forms of colloquial address and greeting. The salutation 'Me Old China' comes from 'china plate' which rhymes with 'mate' for instance!

You might also have wont to address someone as 'Me Old Mucker' – especially a long-time companion or very close friend. It is more a term of familiar endearment addressed to someone who has long shared the travails of life with you. It stems from the expression to 'Muck in' – that is, to take your fair share in all the work that is required to be done, no matter however lowly, however mucky and which includes enduring the 'Muck and Bullets' everyone else has to face! 'Muck and Bullets' is an expression from the trench warfare of the First Great War.

There are also salutations which express familiarity but are not at all intended as terms of endearment. For instance, 'Sunshine' is a term of familiar address but which is used sardonically and sarcastically, to imply or express disdain at someone's actions. Said scornfully, another road user might be addressed thus: "I'm on the right side of the road, Sunshine!" A policeman might, likewise, caution the culprit: "Alright, Sunshine!"

The exclamation, 'Gordon Bennett!' to express surprise or shock was always a familiar and regular retort I used to hear in my youth. When asked, the 'Old Man' (a familiar term for father and husband) would tell me the gentleman concerned was a wealthy American involved in air-balloon racing and all manner of exploits and outrageous behaviour, so much so that he became a veritable household name for anything of that nature that might cause astonishment.

I later discovered for myself that it was he who had sent Stanley on his great quest to find Livingstone! In 1868, the New York Herald journalist, Henry Morton Stanley, set out on his undertaking. The mission was simple and to the point: 'Find Livingstone!' Following up on numerous false trails, reports and rumours, Stanley was almost ready to give up but, finally, travelling into the very depths of darkest Africa, Stanley actually managed to track him down! That now most famous of all journalistic lines, "Dr. Livingstone, I presume?" is almost too matter-of-fact, perhaps, even 'deadpan' in its delivery considering the circumstance and its import, surely, compared with Neil Armstrong's: "One small step for man..!" and outdoes Stanley's by a mile!

'Cockney' was originally a derisory term for a 'Townie' or town dweller. Rhyming Slang typically takes a phrase, the final word of which rhymes with the word that is to be substituted. It is on a par with creating a code by letter

The Rubáiyát of Dinky Dye of Vinegar Yard

substitution! The code word is not the word that rhymes but the initial word in the chosen phrase. Thus so: 'Mince Pies'! I was often being instructed in my youth to 'Open my 'Minces' - my 'Mince Pies' - eyes!

As another example, to be short of a bob or two (a shilling or two) is to be 'Skint' from 'Skinned' which is to be tricked out of your money (and clothes!) by indulging in gambling or being taken advantage of through drink. Sailors on shore leave would find themselves a particular target! My Great Uncle sailed the Seven Seas on the Tall Clipper ships and spent most of his life at sea such that, whenever he stepped back on dry land and came home, he would always descend the stairs backwards!

The slang phrase for 'Skint' is 'Boracic Lint'. Boracic lint is a surgical dressing once in common usage. The code word is 'Boracic' so, if you're 'Boracic' or 'Brassic', you're broke - that is, completely without money or penniless! If you're 'Stone-broke', or just 'Stony', then you really have reached hard times and are 'scraping the bottom of the barrel' - reduced to making best use of the dregs. It could be said you're 'In Queer Street' - in real financial difficulties! A chapter in 'Our Mutual Friend' by Charles Dickens is titled: "Lodgers in Queer Street"!

Another recollection from my youth is my 'Old Lady' (a familiar term for mother and wife) telling me how, before they put in all the modern flood precautions, the Thames would regularly flood their home in Union Street in Southwark. Of course, you might not give a 'Dickey-bird' about that but she and her family certainly did! The phrase,

The Rubáiyát of Dinky Dye of Vinegar Yard

'Couldn't give a Dickey-bird' is used sarcastically, to imply or express a disdain of interest or lack of concern in a matter. You can't be bothered to make even a response or pass any comment whatever in the form of even a single word, or 'Dickey-bird'! What? I never said a 'Dickey-bird' – word!

It might be, if you 'Haven't heard a Dickey-bird' from someone for a while, they might be 'Doing Bird'! That is, 'Bird-lime' or time – 'doing time'! 'Doing time' is to spend a period of time in prison because they've been 'Nicked' – arrested. They might well have been 'Nicked' for being a 'Tea Leaf' – thief! After being 'Nicked', they would have been taken off down to 'The Nick' – police station. Having been found guilty, they would have ended up in 'Nick' – prison – 'Doing Bird'!

A 'nick' is, specifically, a notch of a tally and, having been incarcerated, the prisoner 'Doing Bird' might well want to keep a tally of how many days left to serve in 'Nick'! 'Nicking' was also the practice of clipping or shaving the edges off gold and silver coins to profit from the value of the original coin and accumulate value from the nicks made in the coins. So, if something is in 'Good Nick' it's okay and not noticeably worn away! 'Nicking' is, of course, stealing!

My Uncle Tom was a London Police Constable between the two Great Wars. When being 'Nicked' by the Constable on Patrol (CoP), the 'Tea leaf' might well have been addressed: "You're 'Nicked', 'Sunshine'!" before being read their rights, which only serves to demonstrate, if you don't keep to the straight and narrow, you'll 'Cop it' if you're

The Rubáiyát of Dinky Dye of Vinegar Yard

found out – be punished or spoken to severely because you have done something wrong! Policemen were once called 'Peelers' after the great nineteenth century reformer, Robert Peel, who created the force. They were later called 'Bobbies' for the same reason. There were "Bobbies on bicycles, two by two" in Roger Miller's song, "England Swings"! The Flying Squad, in their sleek, black Wolseley police cars, were called 'The Sweeney' – from Sweeney Todd to rhyme with Squad!

In some parts of London, like the Elephant and Castle, the Constables on Patrol would go out in pairs. To 'Cop' is to seize, to capture, or catch or, in this instance, make an arrest. It might well be the case that the 'Tea leaf' would address the Constable making the arrest – the 'Copper' – with the response: "Fair 'Cop', Guv'nor!" That is, "You caught me fair and square, governor!" 'Guv' or 'Governor' is used also as an informal salutation or means of address or acknowledgement of deference or respect.

My grandad worked as a compositor on Reynolds' Press. On the following page is a sheet from Reynolds' which mentions him and which my 'Old Lady' saved for that very reason. He would bring the paper home, fresh from the print and she would take it outside to read, getting responses like: "'Ow come you got tomorrer's paper?" And that would make her feel especially good. I learnt, also, through my 'Old Lady', as my grandad had informed her, of the reports in the paper, about the dire exploits of the notorious Hoolihan Gang from a lively Irish family of that name in South London and how this was the origin of the word 'Hooligan'.

The Rubáiyát of Dinky Dye of Vinegar Yard

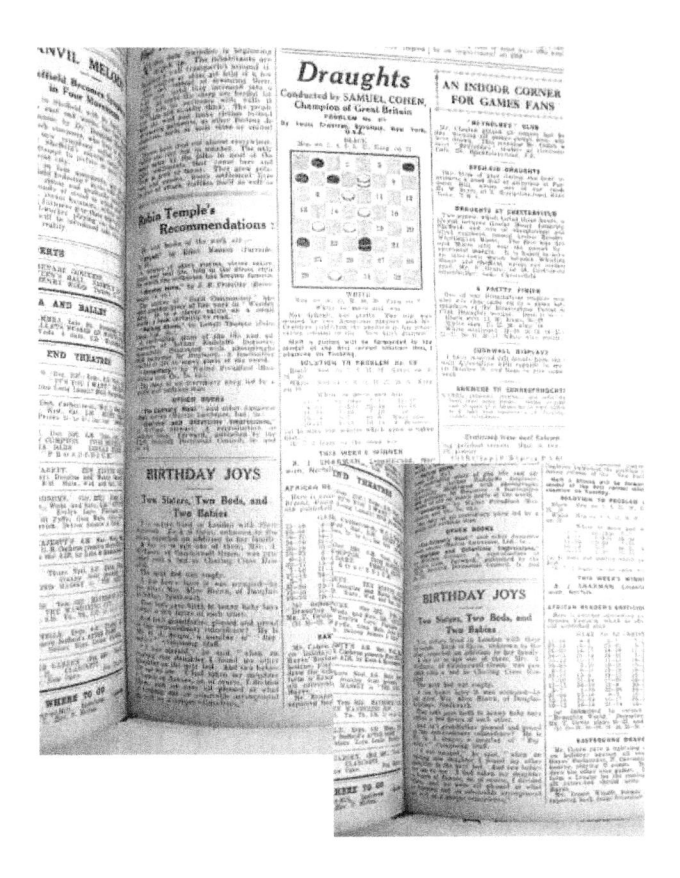

Reynolds, the newspaper's founder and editor, was a Chartist activist and renowned author in Victorian times.

There are many claims for the title 'Real McCoy', even the 'Real MacKay', but I learnt from my 'Old Man' that the expression was actually associated with Canadian, Elijah McCoy's, oil-drip cup invention which he patented in 1872. There were inferior copies around, so railroad engineers, looking to avoid these, would request it by name, inquiring

The Rubáiyát of Dinky Dye of Vinegar Yard

if a locomotive was fitted with "the real McCoy system". There was another claim to the title, more recent. This was from the Prohibition period. Ships under foreign registry ran cargoes up to New Jersey, anchoring outside territorial waters. Many adulterated their contraband with other spirits and dubious substances to further profit from the demand but William McCoy could be counted upon and always reliably delivered the original, untampered goods. Hence: Is it the 'Real McCoy'?

To 'Tip' comes from to tip your hat for a gratuity or an accommodation but, latterly, it has become associated with an acronym – 'To Insure Prompt Service' or 'To Insure Promptness'. The 'Bob' is a slang term for a shilling and comes from 'Bobstick' – a nod to Robert Walpole reducing the Land Tax from four shillings to just one. 'Pound Sterling' comes from a silver Saxon coin called a Sterling. There were 240 Sterlings to one pound in weight of silver and there were 240 pennies to a 'Pound Sterling'. The abbreviation for pound weight is lb, which is an abbreviation of Libra, the Latin for scales, which is also abbreviated to £ which is the monetary pound. The name pound (weight) comes from the 'Pondo' in the Roman measure, Libra Pondo (which was equivalent to nearly 12oz). It was divided into 12 unciae, so a single uncia is roughly the same as an ounce. The abbreviation oz for ounce comes from the Latin word, uncia. Libra is, of course, the sign of the scales in the zodiac!

Many rhyming slang phrases are, perhaps, ironic and logical, as in 'Trouble and Strife' – from the travails of married life – for wife! This is a particular example, among many, where

The Rubáiyát of Dinky Dye of Vinegar Yard

I have only heard the whole phrase used to substitute the target word and not the 'code' word alone. There are some others, such as 'Apples and Pears' – for stairs. Mostly, though, the 'code' word rule stands. So, your 'Barnet' is your head of hair, interchangeable for head and hair, from 'Barnet Fair'! Barnet Fair was the most famous horse fair in England. Barnet, on the main northbound thoroughfare, was known as the town of inns, all taking advantage, no doubt, of the visiting trade. You might well have been asked, while there, to: 'Take a butcher's at this or that horse!' which would be an invitation to: 'Take a look!' The slang here is 'Butcher's Hook' – for look. And more –

Apples and pears – stairs
Cream crackered – knackered (exhausted)
Dog and bone – telephone
Frog and Toad – road
Plates of meat – feet
Whistle and flute – suit

A highlight of our year was always the Boat Race, broadcast on the Home Service. This was the annual Oxford and Cambridge University rowing competition along the tidal stretch of the Thames, between Putney and Chiswick. My 'Old Man' would cheer on Cambridge with me and my 'Old Lady' would cheer on Oxford with my brother, all just for sport and fun! 'Boat Race', of course, is slang for face! 'Put a smile on your boat (race)!'

Apart from being advised to use my 'Minces', I was always being told I should use my 'Loaf'! 'Use your Loaf!' – Loaf

The Rubáiyát of Dinky Dye of Vinegar Yard

of bread: head! Would you 'Adam and Eve' it! – believe it! Use your brain and open your eyes, silly boy! Perhaps, I was 'Doolally' – daft, strange in the head – another word I used to hear frequently. 'Doolally' comes from Deolali, the name of the town where British soldiers were stationed before leaving for home – good old 'Blighty'! Those who became delirious after contracting a fever, or 'Tap' in Hindi, were said to have gone 'Doolally Tap' or 'Doolally'! It's true! I'm not telling 'Porkies' – 'Porky Pies': lies!

Sometimes, the 'code' word may not actually rhyme with but just sound like the target word. So, Joanna sounds like 'Piana' – Piano! My Aunt Ethel could really vamp out a tune on the old Joanna down the 'Rub-a-Dub' – Pub.

When you've got work to get done and it's a hard slog, you soon find out who your 'Muckers' are! Some jobs are quite different, though. Some jobs are really 'Cushy'! "That's a 'Cushy' number you got there!" I confess: I thought this was an extrapolation from 'cushion'. It seemed logical. It seems, though, this is more army slang and derives from the Hindi word 'Khush' meaning happy, easy, content or satisfied and that may explain why my Grandad – respectfully referred to as 'The Old Man' by my 'Old Man' – was oft using it. He was in the army out in India!

Another phrase he used when inviting us to stay over was to get a 'Good Night's Kip' or you can 'Kip Down' here for the night, which, he said, came from keep – sleep – and you have to earn your keep! Since, I've heard it said, it actually has a Scandinavian origin – Norse or Danish – from 'Kippe'

The Rubáiyát of Dinky Dye of Vinegar Yard

My 'Old Lady' said she'd been told my Great Uncle - the one who sailed the Seven Seas! - maintained that it had a nautical origin from Dutch mariners in the Old German word 'Kyppe' (or 'Kippe') for a leather hide stretched out as a makeshift bed - a hammock! Then again, those Danes, like Leif Erickson, were such explorers, perhaps they sailed to India and the word came to us, like so many others, via that route - or perhaps not!

English readily accepts new words - has a voracious appetite for new words - and that may explain why it has become such a Lingua Franca, by adopting foreign words and phrases and being adopted in Pidgin. My 'Old Man' was in the army in North Africa and that explains other acquired slang terms. In English, look how many words and phrases we have for sleep - kip, nap, snooze, doze, nod off, shuteye, drop off, catnap, drift off, bye-byes, dead to the world, in the land of nod, out for the count, bed down, crash out, drop off, flake out, forty winks, get your head down, hit the sack, siesta and *zzzzzzzz*!

In the 1960s, I well remember the 'Hippies' using the term 'Bread' as slang for money. It was widely used and could be heard in such contexts as "I need some bread, man," meaning they were 'Boracic'! The Hippies were largely an American phenomenon but 'Bread', too, is a 'code' word from rhyming slang - 'Bread and Honey' - money! There were also slang terms for money itself, both the struck coinage and paper promissory notes.

The origin of the 'Pound Sterling' has already been mentioned but a pound is also called a 'Quid'. I've also

The Rubáiyát of Dinky Dye of Vinegar Yard

heard it called a 'Squid'! I have been told the slang has applied to other coins of a similar value, like the Guinea and the Sovereign, but I've only heard it used in reference to the Pound. The Guinea and the Sovereign were struck coins, the former being used as the prize in horse races like the 1000 Guineas Stakes run at Newmarket, but the pound was a promissory note. The Guinea, having a value of one Pound and one shilling, and the Sovereign were superior coins, perhaps so because, even if they were 'Nicked', they would still possess real face value!

A 'nick' is, as has been mentioned above, a notch of a tally. A 'notch' in the context of a tally refers to a mark made to keep an account or record of each transaction. Tally sticks were used to record debts incurred and payments made, notched to indicate the amount owed or paid and split in half for both parties to keep as a record of proof of the transactions. If they didn't tally, something would, clearly, be amiss! The 'nick' would stand for a Pound and the 'nicker' – the person marking off the tally – soon became an interchangeable slang term for a Pound – a 'Nicker'.

'Pony' comes from the Hindi word, panja or panje, meaning the five pips or 'five' of a suit of cards and, also, a cast or roll of five of the dice or the 'five' face on a die. A 'Monkey and a Pony' was five hundred and, shortened to a 'Monkey', it was five hundred 'Nicker'. Again, this was from the slang brought back by soldiers and travellers returning from India. An aggregate of five is twenty-five and a 'Pony' came to represent that.

Another word for a 'Nicker' was a 'Oncer' but not once have

The Rubáiyát of Dinky Dye of Vinegar Yard

I heard it applied to a pound coin. Five 'Nicker' is a 'Fiver' and ten is a 'Tenner' and twenty a 'Score'.

Already mentioned, the 'Bob' is a slang term for a shilling and comes from 'Bobstick' - a nod to Robert Walpole. Likewise the 'Tanner' is a slang term for a sixpence and a nod to the Chief Engraver for the Royal Mint who designed it, John Tanner. Back in the days when money was real money - and contained real worth! - the 'Tanner' could be actually bent to make good luck tokens - for a bride's wedding, for instance, or for a token keepsake. I can well remember being invited to stir them into the Christmas pud and make a wish!

The Guinea and the Sovereign were superior coins and out of reach of most. Even sixpences, in their day, were worth a pretty penny, in the context that their value was sufficient enough to be substantial! It was their silver content that enabled them to be bent. Perhaps, that's how the Crooked man found a crooked sixpence! The slang term 'Bender' or 'Going on a Bender' comes from this. A 'Tanner' would be enough and more to see you through for your purchase of drink for a night out on the town!

So, why not half a sixpence - a thruppenny silver 'Joey'! It got its name, Joey, from the fourpenny groat after the coin was discontinued. This had been named Joey after Joseph Hume. Fourpence was the cab fare for short journeys and customers would provide this instead of a 'Tanner' with the customary: "Keep the change!" Being deprived of their 'Tip', the cabbies would offer a 'Fourpenny One' - a physical blow - by way of response, perhaps! The silver

The Rubáiyát of Dinky Dye of Vinegar Yard

thruppenny 'Joey' disappeared from circulation, too, after the war, being then replaced by the twelve-sided brass thruppenny-piece being struck in large numbers.

The performer, Tommy Steele, sang a song of sixpence and good luck tokens (but not a pocketful of rye!) –

> Half a Sixpence
>
> I read in the Sunday papers
> What lover's tokens are
> There's amulets and there's talismans
> Like a ring or a lucky star
> It says that half a sovereign
> Is a thing they use a lot
> But sixpence is the only thing I've got
>
> Still, half a sixpence
> Is better than half a penny
> Is better than half a farthing
> Is better than none
>
> It's a token of
> Our eternal love
> When ya far away
> Touch it everyday

It was only after the war they removed all precious metal content from struck coins in general circulation.

So many words borrowed from the Indian sub-continent! 'Chav' or 'Chavvy' comes from chavani for a cantonment or temporary barracks for troops erected at a military station. If something is basic, really just a roof over your head, it might be described as a bit 'Chavvy' and, likewise, anything – or anyone – common and brash, all dressed up to be what it isn't!

Bandanna is from the Hindi word bandhana meaning to tie or fasten. Bangle has come from bangri, meaning a glass bracelet, and bungalow is from the Hindi word Bangla, a single-storey house built in the Bengal style, which typically included features like verandas and a low-pitched roof.

Chit is from the Hindi word Chitthi meaning a slip of paper, a letter or a note, used in place of money. From the Hindi word Khaat, meaning portable bed or bedstead of the sort soldiers might use in their barracks, comes Cot.

Khaki: An Urdu word meaning dusty or dust coloured has become the adopted colour of a British Army uniform.

Pundit: From the Hindi word Pandit meaning a learned man and the Sanskrit word Panditah meaning learned scholar.

Pyjamas or Pajamas: From the Urdu word payjamah meaning a leg garment.

Shampoo: From the Hindi word Champo, meaning to press and massage.

Thug: From the Hindi word Thag meaning a thief or conman and the Sanskrit word Sthaga meaning robber. The

The Rubáiyát of Dinky Dye of Vinegar Yard

Thuggees were brutal bands of robbers marauding across India engaged in their criminal pursuit. They took the lives of their victims by strangulation and even featured in the film, Indiana Jones!

And that was a brief alphabet of Cockney!

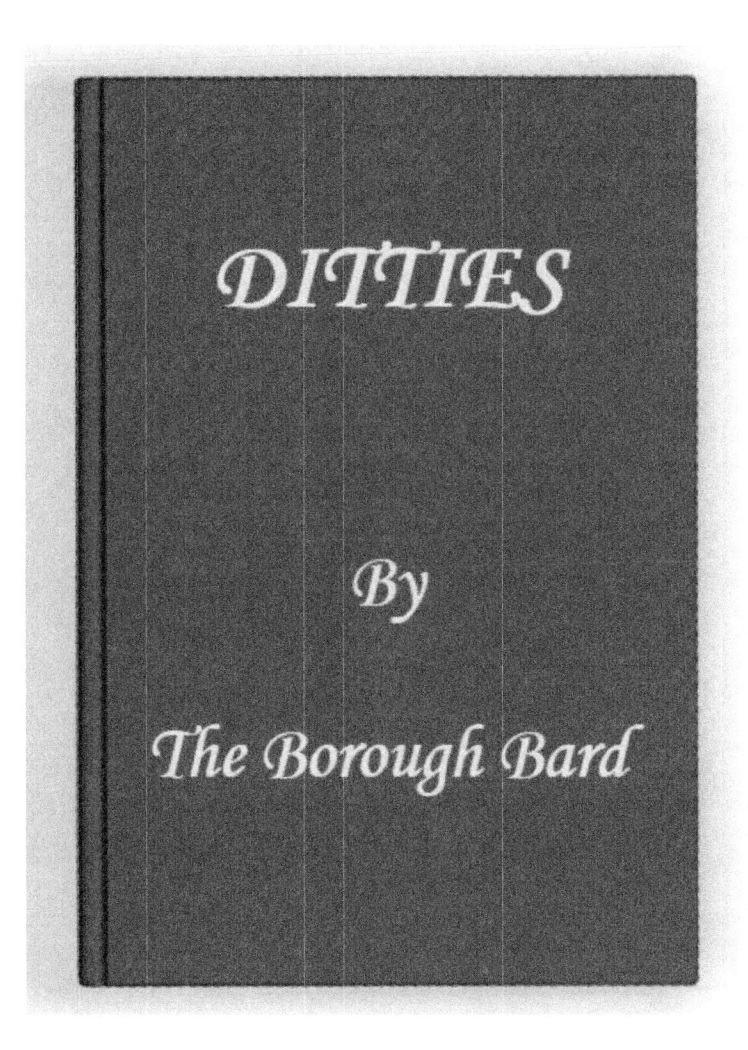

Dinky Dye's Book Of 'Ditties'.

The Rubáiyát of Dinky Dye of Vinegar Yard

The Rubáiyát of Dinky Dye of Vinegar Yard

INDEX OF FIRST LINES

A bitter wine it is to taste of – life! –	37
A blessing, then, upon us both it is –	24
A stolen kiss – how like a dream dreamt 'tis –	33
Abroad the Borough High Street, there, I stroll	24
Across in yon Cathedral grounds, I vouch	23
Ah, foolishness! A heart is not a flower,	31
Ah, leave them with their futile search and come	43
Ah, life is not so easily defined –	42
Ah, not for nothing do you give your love	30
Ah, why must reason from good sense depart	40
Ah, youth is sweet – no more these foul laments –	28
All's but a construct of the mind – just that!	51
Am I a stranger in a stranger's land?	48
And let us leave it better than we find,	27
Another day to do with what we can –	52
As does the vine cleave to the pole, you cleave	32
As morn's chance slingshot glances off St. Paul's,	20
Aye, tap and spile! Small wonder, then, if we	47
Begin each day with kindly thought anew;	53
Beware! Else shall you certain come to grief –	33
But fools believe in love – they will not learn!	37
But let the heart be summoned by desire	39
But love intoxicates as does the vine –	32
But them that claim to be infallible –	28
By choice as much by circumstance they live;	23
Can it be that experience has lied –	41
Day breaks, the market calls and I depart –	19
Death does not leave the last bloom on the stem –	36
Death, that usurper of Life's throne, is chased	36
Deserted is the market, shuttered up,	22
Despite entreaties to him with us while,	47
Do they not say to whistle while you work?	54
First light of morn slinks through the tattered blind –	19

The Rubáiyát of Dinky Dye of Vinegar Yard

First love, first kiss – a dream, a prize to seize –	33
Fool, still does he believe although she lies	40
Fools we must be, then, else we must be mad	41
For Him who judges us, He says we could	35
Frail human flesh we are: we come and go!	34
"God bless you, Guv'nor," is their stock response.	23
Good days, good times, times past and times of ole	26
Hard times some may encounter, some may not:	51
Heed well and take the path that Wisdom takes,	28
How happy I, my produce sold, return	21
How sweet is that first kiss – so does it seem	37
I drew my heavy heart from out my breast	31
I've said my bit; I've said it all and more!	55
If all be well, of good repute our name,	50
If I mistaken am by this or not,	29
In life, do we seek meaning and embark	45
In truth they say, in truth, so it is said:	49
Is love, then, for the simple and naïve?	38
Leave it not so late as this fool has done,	45
Leave not the fancies of the heart to fly	30
Leave them to argue out amongst themselves	42
Life's story can be written on a page –	34
Live life for living's sake and fear not Death,	44
Love and give all the love you have to give;	44
Love, that blind reason of our hearts, invents	38
Mark, when morn comes oft shrouded in a mist,	55
May it be so, a dream, as does it seem?	48
Nay, 'tis not so – good company I share	21
Not mere experience, but wisdom that	29
Now is the time, now is the time to live,	30
Of all the virtues, acts of charity –	24
Of loves sweet memories so few remain –	39
Old Death creeps up on us and, ere our time	35
Old Father Thames, they say, keeps rolling on;	46
Old Father Time, too, marches he along –	46
Once to the wind of love your heart is thrown	34
Ought is there that may last? Nay, there is nought –	22
Sleep on young lovers in your dream of bliss,	38
Small steps lead ever on to greater strides!	25
So poorly our performance is received	35

The Rubáiyát of Dinky Dye of Vinegar Yard

So, too, can it be said for life, that we	41
Some say – "It is not loving that destroys	31
Some say it's so – life is a simple game!	27
Sun, rise; Moon, set: another day begins –	51
The Borough comes alive with commerce and	20
The day's been long and taken of its toll	25
The day's begun cloaked in a shroud of haze –	53
The more I take this maze of life apart,	47
The morn we have been walking has been long;	53
The music of the Market's fresh still in my ear –	26
Their market wares all set out on display,	20
Then, fill my glass again and, one more time,	55
Then, we may know we did our level best	50
Then, what is life: is all for all or nought?	48
There, was it not all worth it? Play your part!	54
There, what know I of this or ought about,	49
Time waits not, cares not, neither deaf nor blind,	49
Time's not misspent – nay, say it isn't so –	27
Times come, times pass, ere done, leave us behind!	46
Until the very end, without regard,	52
What hope is there for us then when a smile	40
What may be so and, to our knowledge, know	50
What merit then is there in wisdom or	42
When life is but a bitter Chalice, then	22
When small ado is much a-being done	21
When that one sends his frenzied pack, his horde	36
When we were young we yearned to be as wise	43
Wherever life leads, there must we be led!	45
While you are young, then, live, enjoy your youth:	43
Whose lips have once desired his truelove's lips;	39
Why this concern with death and human fate	44
With hearty spirit and light-hearted trill,	54
Yes, this one toyed with love and left forlorn	32
Yet, closer do I look, less do I see	26
You see the road before you: then, keep on,	52

Printed in Great Britain
by Amazon